Migrant Farmworkers

A Proud Heritage The Hispanic Library

Migrant Farmworkers

Hoping for a Better Life

Deborah Kent

Content Advisers: Sylvia Partida, Director of Operations
and
Josh Shepherd, Library and Resource Center Manager
National Center for Farmworker Health
Buda, Texas

Published in the United States of America by The Child's World®
PO Box 326 • Chanhassen, MN 55317-0326 • 800-599-READ • www.childsworld.com

Acknowledgments

The Child's World®: Mary Berendes, Publishing Director

Editorial Directions, Inc.: E. Russell Primm, Editorial Director; Pam Rosenberg, Project
Editor; Katie Marsico, Associate Editor; Matt Messbarger, Editorial Assistant; Susan Hindman,
Copyeditor; Lucia Raatma, Proofreader; Stephen Carl Vender, Fact Checker; Timothy Griffin/
IndexServ, Indexer; Dawn Friedman, Photo Researcher; Linda S. Koutris, Photo Selector

Creative Spark: Mary Francis and Rob Court, Design and Page Production

Cartography by XNR Productions, Inc.

Photos

Cover: Migrant farmworkers harvesting chardonnay grapes in Windsor, California, Jim
Sugar/Corbis

AP/Wide World Photos: 14, 15; Barry Sweet/AP/Wide World Photos: 24; Kurt Hegre/The
Fresno Bee/AP/Wide World Photos: 26; Greg Wahl-Stephens/AP/Wide World Photos: 29;
Harry Cabluck/AP/Wide World Photos: 30; Pablo Martinez Monsivais/AP/Wide World
Photos: 34; Bob DeLong/AP/Wide World Photos: 35; Kevin Fleming/Corbis: 7; Vince
Streano/Corbis: 10; Bob E. Daemmrich/Corbis Sygma: 11; Owen Franken/Corbis: 19; Charles
O'Rear/Corbis: 22; Ted Streshinsky/Corbis: 25; Joseph Sohm, ChromoSohm Inc./Corbis: 28;
Danny Lehman/Corbis: 33; Ed Kashi/Corbis: 36; Time Life Pictures/Getty Images: 8, 16, 18,
23; Dorothea Lange/Library of Congress: 9; Library of Congress: 13; Smithsonian Institution,
National Museum of American History: 17; Walter P. Reuther Library, Wayne State University: 21.

Registration

Library of Congress Cataloging-in-Publication Data
Kent, Deborah.
    Migrant farmworkers : hoping for a better life / by Deborah Kent.
        p. cm. — (A proud heritage)
    Includes bibliographical references and index.
    ISBN 1-59296-386-2 (Library Bound : alk. paper) 1. Migrant agricultural laborers—United
States—Juvenile literature. 2. Mexican-American migrant agricultural laborers—Juvenile
literature. I. Title. II. Proud heritage (Child's World (Firm))
    HD1525.K46 2005
    331.5'44'0973—dc22   2004018048

Chapter One

Rules of the Road

"Living this kind of life, there are three things you need to learn," a migrant farmworker told a reporter. "You have to learn not to make long-range plans. You have to be able to pack up and move with just a few hours' notice. And you have to learn to adjust. Adjust to whatever comes along." Migrant workers are workers who take a series of jobs, moving from place to place. Most are employed on farms. They move with the seasons, as new crops are planted or ripen for harvest.

From Maine to California, growers hire millions of migrant farmworkers each year. These workers harvest soybeans in Illinois and pick apples in Washington State. They gather oranges and lemons in Texas and pick grapes, tomatoes, and lettuce in California. When the work is finished on one farm, the migrant farm-workers take new jobs. They may move to the next

Migrant farmworkers harvest tomatoes in Florida.

county, or they may travel halfway across the country
in search of work. As one migrant farmworker explains,
"You're left desperately seeking some way to get money
to support your family. That is the worst feeling, not
knowing where your next paycheck will come from."

When they find work, the migrant farmworkers toil
for long hours in the fields. During the summer, they
do backbreaking work under the blazing sun. In the
fall, they labor in the cold and rain. The pay is low,
and the living conditions can be brutal. In some

Old buses were sometimes used as houses for migrant farmworkers.

places, a shortage of affordable housing forces migrant farmworkers to sleep outdoors on the ground. "They live under bridges or maybe [in] one-room shacks," says Carlos Diaz, director of the Washington Migrant Council. "With the money they earn, they can't afford adequate housing, much less their own place."

Because of their low income, migrant farmworkers can rarely obtain good health care. They may avoid going to the doctor until they are seriously ill. Because they move so often, they cannot always follow up on needed treatment. If tests show that a child should start taking an antibiotic, the family may be gone before the doctor can give them the prescription.

The migrant lifestyle is especially hard on children. It is not unusual for a migrant child to attend three or more schools in a single year. With so many changes, children tend to fall behind in their studies. They also may have trouble making friends. "When we were in Pasco [Oregon], I made a lot of friends," eight-year-old Jimmy Martinez told a newspaper reporter. "But then we left, and I don't think I'll see them again. Now the same thing is going to happen here. It's sad. I don't like to say good-bye."

Many of today's migrant farmworkers are people of Mexican descent who were born in the United States. Many more come to the United States from other countries. They come from

The children of migrant farmworkers must get used to changing schools and leaving their friends each time their families move on to look for work.

Mexicans wait to enter the United States illegally near the border between Mexico and California.

Mexico, Guatemala, El Salvador, and countries in South America. Some come from Jamaica and other Caribbean nations. Some migrant farmworkers come all the way from Asia and the Middle East. Many of these workers enter the country legally, with all of the necessary papers and **permits.** A large number arrive illegally, sneaking across the border without papers. Such illegal migrants are called undocumented aliens.

Why are people willing to journey great distances in order to take difficult, low-paying jobs? Why do farmers hire migrant workers rather than people who live nearby? What can be done to improve living and working conditions for migrant farmworkers? Some of the answers to these questions lie in the history of migrant labor in the United States.

No one knows for certain how many migrant workers are employed in the United States. Migrants move so frequently that they are often missed by **census** takers. Another problem is that undocumented aliens generally avoid talking to researchers. They try to stay away from the authorities for fear of being deported, or sent back, to their country of origin.

Studies suggest that about 81 percent of all migrant farmworkers were born outside the United States. Of these, 77 percent come from Mexico. More than 1 million Mexicans do migrant agricultural work on U.S. farms. Almost one-half of all migrant farmworkers born in the United States are people of Latino heritage.

Migrant farmworkers are relatively young. Two-thirds of them are under the age of 35. In 1997, 6 percent of this workforce consisted of children under 17.

Chapter Two

Helping Hands

In 1877, a cruel dictator named Porfirio Díaz came to power in Mexico. Under Díaz's rule, wealthy landowners expanded their estates by taking land from the poor. The peasants, or *campesinos,* were forced to work on large ranches for pitifully low wages.

Life in Mexico offered little hope. Across the Rio Grande, however, lay the United States, where there were jobs on railroads, ranches, and farms. By Mexican standards, these jobs paid well. Mexican campesinos began making the journey north to take jobs in the United States. By crossing the border, they reached for a better life. Some of these workers made the United States their permanent home. Others worked for a while, saved money, and returned to Mexico.

After 30 years under Díaz's leadership, Mexico exploded into a revolutionary war in 1910. The

Mexican Revolution (1910-1920) was bloody and chaotic. To escape this turmoil, thousands of Mexicans migrated to the United States, where farms and factories had a steady need for willing hands. The Mexicans were happy to fill this need.

In general, the Mexicans received far less pay than did American-born workers. Some people complained that migrant workers took jobs away from Americans, who demanded higher wages.

A soldier prepares for battle during the Mexican Revolution.

13

A U.S. Border Patrol inspector checks train compartments in 1951.

In addition, many white Americans felt uneasy around the dark-skinned strangers from across the border. They insisted that the United States would soon be overrun by Spanish-speaking immigrants. In 1924, the federal government created the U.S. Border Patrol. Armed guards along the 2,000-mile (3,200 kilometer) United States–Mexico border tried to stop Mexicans from crossing illegally into the United States. People from Mexico could enter only with papers issued by the U.S. government.

When the United States entered World War II (1939–1945) in 1941, thousands of men and women left the farms to join the military. Factories also recruited farmworkers to build planes, tanks, and warships. The United States had a sudden need for workers to tend the fields. In 1942, the United States and Mexico signed an agreement called the Bracero Treaty. The treaty created a program that permitted Mexicans to work in the United States under contract. In Mexico, campesinos signed up to do farm work in the United States for a given period of time and for a set wage. For the campesinos, the Bracero Program looked like a glorious opportunity.

Helping Hands

The term bracero comes from the Spanish word *brazo,* meaning arm. The strong arms of the braceros were wanted in the United States. For some reason, non-Hispanic Americans believed that bracero meant helping hand. During World War II, the braceros were sometimes called helping hands from Mexico.

Migrant farmworkers from Mexico wait in line for job interviews in California in 1959.

The Bracero Program continued long beyond the close of the war. It operated from 1942 until 1964. During that time, more than 4 million Mexican farmworkers—nearly all of them men—entered the United States. Depending on his contract, a bracero might work from a few months to several years before returning to Mexico.

Most braceros worked on farms in California and the Southwest. They had worked the land back in Mexico, and they brought years of experience to their jobs in the United States. They were not afraid to work hard or to put in long hours.

When they weeded lettuce, sugar beets, and many other crops, the braceros used a tool called the short-handle hoe. In Spanish, they called it *el cortito,* or the little shorty. Because the handle was only 12 to 18 inches long (30 to 46 centimeters), the worker had to bend over almost halfway to the ground to use the hoe. "In the evenings I would unbend myself and see my hands swollen because all the blood had rushed

downward," remembered a former bracero named Hisauro Reyes. Farmers often refused to let their workers use long-handle hoes that would have allowed them to stand upright. Farmers claimed that the long-handle hoe would damage the crops. Today, the short-handle hoe has been outlawed in most states.

The braceros made a tremendous contribution to American agriculture. Nevertheless, non-Hispanic Americans tended to look down upon them. They saw the braceros as dirty and uneducated. In 1948, a writer described how braceros were treated in Texas. "[The bracero] is regarded as a necessary evil. . . .

Many movie theaters required braceros to sit in separate sections.

One might assume that he is not a human being at all, but a species of farm **implement** [tool] that comes into being with the maturing of the cotton." When they went into town, braceros were greeted by signs that stated No Mexicans Allowed. Cafés refused to serve them. In movie theaters, they had to sit in a special section. They were even forbidden to use most public restrooms.

Compared to wages in Mexico, the pay that

the braceros received was decent. By U.S. standards, however, their wages were miserable. During the 1950s, braceros in California earned 60 cents an hour. They received only 30 cents an hour in Texas. Ten percent of the worker's wages was held for him in Mexico. Supposedly he would receive this money when he crossed back over the border. However, few braceros ever managed to collect these withheld wages.

Many Mexicans come to the United States hoping to escape the poverty they face in their home country.

The flow of workers from Mexico to the United States went on, even after the Bracero Program ended. Poverty was widespread in Mexico. In the United States, jobs were plentiful. In the farming industry, employers still depended on the helping hands of Mexican workers. Sometimes legally, sometimes without papers, workers from Mexico continued to cross the border.

Chapter Three

"United We Stand"

On November 25, 1960, the CBS television network aired the documentary *Harvest of Shame.* The film revealed the horrific living and working conditions of migrant fruit pickers in Florida. The voices of farmworkers poured into comfortable living rooms across the country. Viewers could not forget the bent backs, gnarled hands, and careworn faces of the men, women, and children portrayed on the screen. For the first time, the public became aware of the migrant farmworkers' plight. Yet, for the migrant farmworkers, nothing changed.

Early in the 20th century, factory workers in U.S. cities had organized into trade **unions.** By acting together through the unions, they pushed for better pay and improved working conditions. Farmworkers, however, had not become unionized. Because they were widely scattered and moved often, it was hard

César Chávez (far right) stands with other National Farm Workers Association organizers at the NFWA founding convention.

for them to organize. Without a union, they had no way to work as a group and press for change.

In 1962, César Chávez, a former migrant farmworker, established a farmworkers' union in California. It was called the National Farm Workers Association until 1972, when it became known as the United Farm Workers Association (UFWA). In the beginning most UFWA members worked in California's vineyards. They tended and harvested table grapes and grapes used in the making of wine. Work in the vineyards was hard, hot, and exhausting. One journalist wrote: "The workers hunch under the vines like ducks. There is no air, making the intense heat all but unbearable. Gnats and bugs swarm out from under the leaves." Poisonous black widow spiders lurked among bunches of grapes, ready to bite an unwary hand. There were no bathroom facilities in the fields. The growers provided drinking water, but the workers had to buy every

A farmworker harvests grapes from a vine in Oregon.

César Chávez was born in 1927 near Yuma, Arizona. When he was 11, his family moved to California and began to work in the fields. For years, Chávez followed the harvests up and down the state. Later, he dedicated his life to helping migrant farm-workers push for better wages and working conditions. "If you're outraged at conditions," Chávez once said, "then you can't possibly be free or happy until you devote all your time to changing them." Chávez died in 1993 after a lifetime of devotion to the farmworkers' cause.

cupful. Often, the workers were exposed to pesticides that the growers sprayed on the crops to kill bugs. For all of their efforts, the workers were paid only a dollar an hour.

A group of Filipino grape pickers near Delano, California, went on strike in September 1965. Within days, the UFWA joined the strike. Striking farmworkers formed **picket lines** around the vineyards. The strikers carried signs and chanted slogans. Some of the signs read United We Stand. The growers were furious. They threw mud at the strikers and even threatened to shoot them. Chávez warned the strikers not to fight back. He knew they would gain the public's respect if they remained peaceful but firm.

César Chávez joins other farmworkers during the California grape boycott in 1966.

As the weeks passed, thousands of volunteers aided the strikers. They raised money to support families who were staying out of the fields. They also helped organize a nationwide **boycott** of products made by Schenley Industries, a major Delano grape producer. Most of Schenley's profits came from the sale of alcoholic beverages.

Striking California farmworkers march from Delano to Sacramento in 1966.

The strikers and their supporters urged the public not to buy Schenley products until the company **negotiated** with the UFWA. Millions of Americans supported the strike by refusing to buy beverages with the Schenley label. As the strike went on, Schenley lost more money each day.

The strike and the boycott continued through the winter. At last, Schenley agreed to negotiate with the UFWA. Schenley raised the farmworkers' wages to $1.35 an hour and promised to hire union members in the future.

A black eagle, the symbol of the United Farm Workers Association, on a flag carried by a worker at a rally in California in 2003.

Schenley was only one of many large grape growers. The UFWA kept up the pressure on the others. The boycott of California grapes even extended overseas. In Europe, dockworkers refused to unload California grapes from American ships. By the end of 1967, the strike had cost the growers more than $25 million.

More and more growers negotiated with the union. When a company negotiated a contract with the UFWA, it could put the union symbol, a black eagle, on its boxes of grapes. The public knew that grapes with the black eagle were not under the boycott. As a result of César Chávez's work, conditions for vineyard workers improved. Workers received better pay and more effective protection from pesticides. The growers paid into a fund to provide retirement and health benefits.

The impact of the UFWA reached beyond the vineyards. In 1966, workers in the melon fields of South Texas went out on strike. Thousands of melon workers marched to Austin, the state capital, to meet with legislators. Despite strong public support, however, the melon workers' strike was unsuccessful. The growers replaced the striking workers with scabs, nonunion men and women willing to work in spite of the strike. Most of the scabs came from Mexico. The growers

The Texas state capitol, built in 1888, was modeled after the U.S. Capitol in Washington, D.C.

knew that the Mexicans were desperate for work and would accept almost any conditions.

Although not all strikes were successful, the public grew increasingly aware of migrant farmworkers and their needs. By the 1990s, some **exemplary** programs were created to improve their standard of living. State and federal laws required growers to provide bathroom facilities in fields where more than 10 migrant farmworkers were working. Some growers and farming communities built new housing for migrants. Public health nurses visited migrant families. When families moved on to the next harvest, clinics would send their medical records along to the next facility.

Schools developed special programs to help migrant children catch up with their classmates. In 1972, Saint Edward's University in Austin, Texas,

Health care workers review a patient's chart at La Clinica del Carino, a clinic that serves migrant farmworkers in Hood River, Oregon.

The director of the migrant student assistance program at Saint Edward's University poses with a student in 2003.

pioneered a scholarship program for students from migrant families. Other colleges and universities have followed suit.

Migrant families still face many hardships. Many growers provide very poor living conditions. Health care and educational opportunities remain inadequate for many farmworker families. Yet workers from Mexico and other nations continue to flock to the United States, eager to find work in the fields.

Chapter Four

Crossing to El Norte

In 1994, the U.S. government built a 12-foot-high (3.6-meter-high) steel fence along several miles of the United States–Mexico border east of San Diego, California. Similar fences appeared in Texas near El Paso and McAllen. These fences were designed to keep Mexican immigrants from illegally entering the United States.

Government officials hoped this would make work lighter for the Border Patrol. The United States spends billions of dollars a year in its efforts to keep illegal immigrants from entering the country. Despite these massive efforts, people from Mexico continue to enter the United States, with or without papers, in search of work.

Crossing to *el norte*—the north—can be expensive and dangerous. Most people trying to sneak across the border hire an experienced guide known as a **coyote.**

Though crossing the border between Mexico and the United States illegally can be dangerous and expensive, many Mexicans attempt it each year. The desire to find work and a better life in the United States outweighs their fear.

A coyote usually charges between $1,000 and $5,000 to bring someone into the United States. He shows the traveler where and how to cross the Rio Grande, and helps that person dodge the Border Patrol. Anyone caught will be held in **detention** or sent back to Mexico.

Hundreds of immigrants died in accidents or in shoot-outs with the Border Patrol between 1995 and 2000. One man, Hisauro Reyes, described swimming across the Rio Grande: "What a river that is! Why, it's gobbled up a lot of Mexicans! Its waters go in a swirl, like a whirlpool. You mustn't swim strongly. You must swim relaxed, because if you don't you'll tire, and the water grabs you and takes you all the way to the bottom."

The Immigration and Reform Act of 1986 granted **amnesty** to some 3 million illegal immigrants. About 90 percent of them were from Mexico and other countries in Latin America. The act allowed these people to gain legal status and apply to become U.S. citizens. At

Mexicans cross the Rio Grande to enter the United States illegally.

President George W. Bush spoke about immigration in 2004.

the same time, the law tried to prevent more people from arriving illegally and getting jobs. It imposed heavy fines on employers who hired undocumented aliens. The fines were seldom enforced, however, and undocumented immigrants continued to arrive.

In 2004, President George W. Bush proposed a new immigration law. The law would allow undocumented workers to stay in the United States for up to three years. At the end of that time, they would have to return to their homeland. They would collect a portion of their pay when they re-entered their native country. "This program will be more humane to workers and will live up to the highest ideals of our nations," Bush stated. Those who remembered the Bracero Program had grave doubts. "How can they create another program, when they still haven't paid the debt to the braceros?" asked the daughter of a bracero who never received his payment when he returned to Mexico in the 1950s.

The conditions that brought the braceros to the United States have changed very little. Jobs remain scarce in Mexico, and employers in the United States are still hungry for cheap labor. This is especially true in the farming industry, where growers employ large work crews at certain peak times. Much of that work-force is supplied by immigrants from Mexico.

Sending Home a Paycheck

Sometimes a farmworker in Texas or California is the sole supporter of his family back home. Immigrant workers send billions of dollars to their families in Mexico each year. "It feels very good to be paid, but it feels even better when I send money home," one migrant said in an interview. "Then I say to myself, 'I have done something!'"

A migrant worker family watches TV at their home in California.

Migrant workers have endured hunger, pain, exhaustion, and prejudice in the United States. Despite these hardships, immigrants continue to cross the border to take jobs in the fields. America remains the land of hope. In the United States, one's children and grandchildren have a chance at a better life. "They will never be able to prevent entry into the United States from our country," one migrant told a reporter. "As long as hope is there for something better, we will find a way."

1877: Porfirio Díaz, a cruel dictator, becomes president of Mexico. Wealthy landowners begin taking land from the poor.

1910: A revolution breaks out in Mexico, leading to 10 years of bloodshed and chaos.

1924: The U.S. Border Patrol is created to prevent undocumented aliens from entering the country.

1941: The United States enters World War II. Thousands of men and women leave farms to work in factories.

1942: An agreement between Mexico and the United States establishes the Bracero Program.

1960: CBS airs *Harvest of Shame,* a documentary on migrant fruit pickers.

1962: César Chávez founds the United Farm Workers Association (UFWA) in California.

1964: The Bracero Program ends.

1965: The UFWA launches a strike against California grape growers.

1966: Melon workers in South Texas go on strike and march to the state capitol.

1972: Saint Edward's University in Austin, Texas, begins a scholarship program for students from migrant families.

1986: The Immigration and Reform Act grants amnesty to illegal immigrants.

1993: César Chávez dies.

2004: President George W. Bush proposes a new program that would allow undocumented workers from Mexico to work for limited periods in the United States.

amnesty (AM-nuh-stee) To grant someone amnesty is to promise not to punish that person for having broken the law. When undocumented aliens are granted amnesty, they can work in the country legally.

boycott (BOI-kot) During a boycott, the public supports a strike by refusing to buy a company's products. The UFWA organized a nationwide boycott of California grapes.

census (SEN-suss) A census is an official count of the people living in a country. Migrants move so frequently that they are often missed by census takers.

coyote (kye-OH-tee) A coyote is a guide hired to help people cross illegally from Mexico to the United States. A coyote may charge $1,000 to help someone sneak into the country.

detention (di-TEN-shun) People who are held in detention are kept as prisoners until the date of their hearing, or trial. People caught trying to cross the border illegally will be kept in detention or sent back to Mexico.

exemplary (eg-ZEM-pluh-ree) Something that is exemplary deserves to be imitated because of its excellence. Some exemplary programs were created to improve the migrant farmworkers' standard of living.

implement (IM-pluh-muhnt) An implement is a tool. The short-handle hoe is a farming implement.

negotiated (ni-GOH-shee-ate-id) To have negotiated means to have bargained. After a long strike, Schenley Industries agreed to negotiate with the UFWA.

permits (PUR-mits) Permits are papers that allow a person to perform an activity such as driving or working. A legal immigrant has the necessary permit to work.

picket lines (PIK-it LINEZ) Picket lines are lines of strikers at a work site. The UFWA strikers formed picket lines around the vineyards.

unions (YOON-yuhnz) Unions are organizations of workers that enable them to bargain for better wages and working conditions. César Chávez founded the United Farm Workers Association, a union for farmworkers.

Books

Ancona, George. *Harvest*. New York: Marshall Cavendish, 2001.

Gaines, Ann. *César Chávez: The Fight for Farm Workers' Rights*. Chanhassen, Minn.: The Child's World, 2003.

Krull, Kathleen. *Harvesting Hope: The Story of César Chávez*. New York: Harcourt Brace, 2003.

Murcia, Rebecca Thatcher. *Dolores Huerta*. Bear, Del.: Mitchell Lane Publishers, 2003.

Web Sites

Visit our home page for lots of links about migrant farmworkers:

http://www.childsworld.com/links.html

Note to Parents, Teachers, and Librarians:
We routinely check our Web links to make sure they're safe, active sites—
so encourage your readers to check them out!

About the Author

Deborah Kent was born in Glen Ridge, New Jersey, and grew up in nearby Little Falls. She graduated from Oberlin College and received a master's degree from Smith College School for Social Work. For four years, she was a social worker at University Settlement House on New York's Lower East Side. In 1975, Ms. Kent moved to San Miguel de Allende in Mexico, where she wrote her first young-adult novel, *Belonging*. While in San Miguel, Ms. Kent helped to found the Centro de Crecimiento, a school for children with disabilities. Ms. Kent is the author of numerous young adult novels and nonfiction titles for children. She lives in Chicago with her husband, children's author R. Conrad Stein, and their daughter, Janna.